If I Should Die Before I Wake

Gregory Edward Douglas

Pegasus Books
8165 Valley Green Drive
Sacramento, CA 95823
www.pegasusbooks.net

First Edition: January 2022

Published in North America by Pegasus Books. For information, please contact Pegasus Books c/o Marcus McGee, 8165 Valley Green Drive, Sacramento, CA 95823.

Library of Congress Cataloguing-In-Publication Data
Gregory Edward Douglas
If I Die Before I Wake/ Gregory Edward Douglas – 1st ed.
p. cm.
Library of Congress Control Number: 2010943597
ISBN – 978-1-941859-85-8
1. POLITICAL SCIENCE / Civil Rights. 2. POLITICAL SCIENCE / Political Ideologies. 3. SOCIAL SCIENCE / African American Studies.4. SOCIAL SCIENCE / Discrimination. 5. POLITICAL SCIENCE / Public Policy / Social Policy.

10 9 8 7 6 5 4 3 2 1

Comments about *On the Other Side of This Reality* and requests for additional copies, book club rates and author speaking appearances may be addressed to Pegasus Books c/o Gregory Edward Douglas, or you can send your comments and requests via e-mail to gregdouglas767@icloud.com.

Also available as an eBook from Internet retailers and from Pegasus Books

Printed in the United States of America

Dedication

"If I Should Die Before I Wake, I Pray the Lord My Soul To Take..."

Eventually To Join These Giants
Whose FootSteps
May Have Been Silent
But Whose Souls Were
Strong And Reliant
Enough To Lift
Such A Heavy Head
To Face This World
Before I Went To Bed...

PROPS:

Mary Elizabeth Douglas, Rose Green, Pearl Douglas, Clifford Brown, Norma Ragland, Morris Wood, Beth White, Josiah Wallace, Steve Mark, Momma Bishop, Anne Schwerner, Floyd Fleming, Verta Jean, James Robinson, Marcellus Toney, James Alan Keyes, Donnie Edons, Bobbie Gunn, Herman Kelsaw, Bubba Washington, Louis Derry, Austin Charity, Ethel Parker, Elizabeth McBride, Fannie Lou Hamer, Sam Gibson, Coreen Charity, Ora Brown, Josephine Jones, Momma: Ethel Wallace, Ona Neal, Constance Stewart, Nate Walker, Edward Matthews Douglas and those yet to find that compassion

gregoryedouglas

seven/three/cleareyesight

Introduction

When I was very young, my mother, before going to work at night, would always have me drop to my knees and recite the prayer, "Now I Lay Me Down to Sleep." As many times as I have prayed as a child, I never did really think of the full scope of *if I should die before I wake.* Other than the plea for The Master to carry me off to Heaven, I thought nothing of what or whom I'd be leaving behind. Now that I'm much, much older, somewhere during the aging process, I gravitated to "The Lord's Prayer," which doesn't address "If I should die before I wake?"

What merits one's ascension? Most assuredly, it must involve the love that we have for our family and fellow man/woman and the actions that we take to insure their wellbeing. But life's road is never smooth and differences in its bumps and the degree of its grades spawn difficulties that are reflected in attitudes which we must identify and cope within our attempts to overcome.

In doing our best, we win a few and lose a few, but we are always trying. This life will eventually go on without us. Yes, we will all fall victim in that trail dust of the past. If I should die before I wake may this serve as a footnote, or a small keepsake, donated to verify that, regardless of the attitudes, bumps, victories, ties or unlikely outcomes, that I was here...

Gregory E. Douglas

If I Should Die Before I Wake

If I Should Die Before I Wake

List of Poems

In The Blink of God's Eyes

May He in His Time

Help Us to Bridge

This Viral Death Spiral

For Life

Can't Really Be Itself Again

Not Even Close –

Without You...

gregorye.douglas

four/twenty-three twenty/clearsight

The Masters of Our Fates

Untreated
Diabetes leads to Amputations
Hypertension To Heart Attacks and Strokes
Drug Addiction to Overdoses
Alcohol Leads to Cirrhosis
Emphysema From Dust and Smoke

The Covid 19 Virus Vaccines
As effective as they have been
Are objected to by far too many
When asked the reason why
There isn't any

No Masks No Distance & No Vaccines
All so they can appear free
In a land of 700 thousand deaths
It causes you to hold your breath
As the caskets mount around me

Covid 19 like smog – now scours our cities,
Sticking to skin and clothes
Or passed on by a handshake or doorknob
Or cough droplets entering your nose
And as sturdy as you may feel

Like Velcro, it comes to attach and steal
Whatever it can from whomever it will
Vaccines are there to set up defenses
To uphold our census by avoiding consequences
Brothers, sisters, moms or dads – it takes whomever
it wants
Without vaccines this viral fiend just hunts and
hunts and haunts...

gregorye.douglas
eight/twenty-four/cleareyesight/plusone

The Soul Has No Color,

But Survives as a Victim

Of The Hue It Inherits

gregorye.douglas

nine/thirteen/cleareyesight

Black Life 101

If the night hasn't
Held you hostage
And a fresh chill
Disturbs your face

If you can in the mornings
Lift those heavy lids
And without a warning
Find the gift of sight to embrace

If you can raise your chest
To permit your lungs
Precious air to invest
Before falling back into place

Then
You have a chance...

gregorye.douglas
two/twenty-three/cleareyesight/plusone

As Fixed as We Are

days transitioned
one into the other
from sunup to sundown
compiling years of neglect
stacking decades upon decades
to erect the centuries of shadow people
left to germinate solely from their own darkness

from days somehow transitioned
ole sol's full noontime glare
no longer causes a constant squinting
for the truth nor shields transparency
it now exposes and confirms the indictment
of how consistently cruel Black life really is – Still

Principally because the system has a
commitment and devotion
to exert control and sequentially
contort the neck
    of the hourglass
    to rob democracy of time
    and us of our next breath

gregorye.douglas
four/eleven/cleareyesight/plusone

If You Had a Choice of Colors...

It's amazing how everyone finds
greens and blues and hazels
So startling
It's enough to make them stop
To appreciate these life colors
That settle into the iris of the eye
But never bleed into the skin
And what if they did?
What, then, would be our regard?
Simply friendly, or alien?
And what if purely whites or purely Blacks?
Certainly colors that the iris lacks...

gregorye.douglas
four/eleven/cleareyesight/plusone

Slavery

Through the bone

Straight to the marrow

A cry is heard from a sparrow

Trapped by bars so very narrow

Yet its pain can be heard

Over the melody of this caged bird

Whose message may find no home

gregorye.douglas

seven/three/2016/cleareyesight/plusone

Penned Up Like Lab Rats

Propagating Neurosis

Ghettos In Lock-Down

Acid Rain

Witness to this freak occurrence
No shelter from this acid rain
A high wire act on a razors edge
While elephants trample upon my brain

Thirsting for the staple needed
The dollar now has superseded
Love from which we did feed it
Was our bread and water

Labor's mechanical monotony
Like raindrops pinging in my ears
Echoing long after the door closes
Hermetically sealing in my fears

Love's shower has less zeal
Lost its appeal
Less of me no longer there
Leaving this ghost to consider the woes
Of the endless redlines that we toe

Life's futility mocks me
A repetition of yesterday
Slipping in mid-uphill grade

Leaving body horizontal
Head extended eyes straight up and my
assurance frayed
A pallbearer in life's procession
Eventual subject in death's parade

Love's residue is bequeathed in my 9 to 5
Bent on holding the line
Reward: needing 100 yet receiving 99
Pachyderms still pounce and cerebral spasms
linger on
Muscles remain in tetanic contractions
This acid rain is never gone

gregorye.douglas
four/eighteen/zero four

The Bloody Truth

(BOBC)

Night Lights In Ghettos
Signals of life flashes
Shadows disguise the living and dead
Deliberating until someone arises or something finally is said

Blinded brainless ambition wages wars
Ghetto rites and victories largely go ignored
How shallow each outcome, yet one by one,
They come to be gored

Beautifully bronzed breathless bodies
Statued black toreadors are fitted for graves
Painfully others mindlessly enlist
For tomorrows corrida (death march) already enslaved

Armistice promises not to appear
Til the last hymn's "amen" is sung
Or the rats finally find an ear
And yell to the top of their lungs
For the terrors to disappear...

gregorye.douglas
eleven/ten/2015

Airs Current Heirs

clinging to this precipice
racism's impending weight rests
on this country's integrity
while examining the capacity
of our faith's endurance
perched and waiting for any assurance

Entrusting this global burden
To minds rutted in yesterdays
Now to pennae volatus & young fledgings' faith
That in one leap are destined to become
The maiden flight or martyred failures
It matters how the air is won

r.i.p.:GF
gregorye.douglas
four/twenty/cleareyesight/plusone

Spring

Will Spring Ever Come Fast Enough

Will It Ever Last long Enough

To Make Us Tough Enough

To Last And Love Til Another Spring

As With Others – That's The Thing...

gregoryedouglas
twelve/twenty-nine/cleareyesight

I Begged On My Knees

Although I Had More To Give

You Had More To Lose...

TJ's Lovers
Lost And Found
Collection

Love Illogic

It was awkward – to discover

That you touched me like no other

And then you found another lover

Now I'm touched in different way

T'l Neruda

Love Ghost

We all remember

What lovers gave

And certain aspects

We'd like to save

And here's where

Memories appear so grave

Like your perfume

Floating through this room

In another time to exhume

These hauntings

T'l. Neruda

Love Amnesia

I've tried to forget
The way you walk
The fullness of your lips
The way you talk
The surprised expression on your face
How you feel and how you taste
The way you act
When you are smug
Your loving arms
The way they hug
The way I felt
Each time we met
The love you gave
And I gave to you
The love I've saved
Since we were through
Yes for you
I've tried to forget...
T'J. Neruda

Love Azul

Sometimes

I think of you

And some of the things

We used to do

And then the color

Fades to blue

And I'm alone again

T'i. Neruda

As If You Didn't Know ...

You are my air
Or I couldn't conceive
Of what you think
Or what to believe
Of how to act or what to say
About the art of living
And its complex ways
When at last we have the time
To talk of life and how it winds
With hands in hands and nose to nose
It matters not how harsh winds blow

It matters more that this love grows
Through all of the blossoms
And the thorns of the rose
At night when all colors fade
Our greatest dreams
May remain in their graves
Some lost in darkness
Others exhumed by day

Where your greatest flaw
Is never onyx laden skin
It's holding your breath
When I need your wind

gregorye.douglas
two/fourteen/cleareyesight

The Shiva Exponent

As Prematurely As The Sun
Saps This Weary Back
So Life Leaves Me Another Incremental Death
The Passage of Time Without You

Memories of our Love's Brief Enchantment
Lay Sealed and Buried in a Time Capsule that
With my Greatest wish and in my Weakest hour
Cannot Open to Find You Whole and Well Again

Was I not worthy enough to Have Loved You Forever
Or Within this Galaxy for a Lightyear
Or at Least until Spring
Seasons Life's Renaissance

Lodged At the Mouth of My Brain
This "Oppressive Loss Obsession" Finds Its Liberty
Barricading Thoughts Blockading Dreams
Torturing this Soul Imprisoning The Body
Oh, The Guilt in Loss!
A Mind This Dedicated Is Never Free
And Transfixes Me Here at This Post

gregorye.douglas
twelve/twenty-seven//cleareyesight/plusone

Life

Is the Canvas

In Which We Live

In Reds. Blues, Blacks and Tears

gregorye.douglas

twelve/ten/cleareyesight/plusone

Texture of the Truth

When Black Men lie
They are incarcerated

When White Men lie
They are exonerated

gregorye.douglas
nine/ten/cleareyesight

Like Raindrops
Pelting The Marble Floor

In This Country
The Only Reason Why We Don't Have Gun Control
Is Because of the Immense Pleasure
We Derive From
Killing One Another

In This Country
The Other Reason Why We Don't Have Gun Control
Is Because of the Immense Pleasure
Others Derive from Watching

In This Country
Another Reason Why We Don't Have Gun Control
Is Because Technology Has Out-Paced
Human Development Meaning
Trigger Fingers Aren't Amputated...

gregorye.douglas
five/twenty-eight/cleareyesight/plusone

Is Isn't Ain't

Was it said
Was it spoken
Was it heard
Was it inferred
Was it interpreted
Was it translated

Better that it was written
Aged forever in ink
Dyed on the parchment
That died a friendship
One thought everlasting
One ephemeral thought – the other

Wounded skewed and severed
Insidious silence seize
The only life that remains
Time has nourished this cancer
And grown this crop for harvest
Which is only suited for a devil's feast

gregorye.douglas
eleven/ nine/ 2017

Trumphant

On January 6, 2021

While Justice slept and Lincoln wept

The injured and dead were being swept

By most Republicans under the carpet

After January 6, 2021

Fear blood and caskets bred on the Capitol Floor

Treasures from Trumps followers brought straight through the doors

Leaving these stained hallways as souvenirs for ghosts and forevermore

gregory.douglas
two/fourteen/cleareyesight/plusone

The Zoo with a View

In D.C. yesterday for all the world to see
Was a horde of trump's redheaded monkeys
Using the Capitol as their tree

They overpowered the Capitol Guards
Who looked anemic without riot gear
One has to wonder
Why there were even there

trump's redheaded monkeys climbed the stairs
While others scaled the walls
The electoral college was unaware
Of the breach and the brawls

Successfully breaking and entering
These monkeys flooded the halls
Destroying a lot of property
Leaving Congress to scurry for safety
And The Electoral Count was stalled

Such an outrageous act of sedition yesterday
On display at the Capitol DC Zoo
Spawned by trump's pep talk
That opened their cages for all ages to view

With so little resistance and so much force
Though anticipated we all know
Pigments are never dismissed from a mess like this while
Justice always seems in recess –
Exclusively for the Albinos

gregoryedouglas
one/seven/cleareyesight/plus one

Who Chose The Black Doll

Derek Chauvin's
Defense Attorney during George Floyd's trial
Asked why didn't the onlookers
Try to step in and help Mr. Floyd?
The more intelligent question was
Why didn't Derek Chauvin's fellow officers,
Who didn't seem annoyed?
And in full view could see Floyd
Under Chauvin's knee chokehold,
Why didn't they react
To pull Chauvin off
To save poor George in fact?

Because if those unarmed onlookers
Had rushed to Mr. Floyd's defense,
Brothers & Sisters coming to George's aid
Would have been applauded for all the help they gave
Wouldn't have been arrested
Not even molested
They would have been allowed

To leave the breached Capitol to go home...

Snap !

They all would have been slaughtered
At the sight of George's Minneapolis Misery Demise
Because in plain sight
And with clear skies,
Cops kill Black People,
Yeah, they do
The D.C. Guard
Pleaded ignorance & impotence
As concert goers jumped the Capitol fence
And as trump had them all hyped He did
The Conservative Caucasian Offense made their bid
And after limited seating and a couple of beatings
Everyone went home
Yeah, they did!

gregorye.douglas
four/nine/cleareyesight/plusone

Memorial Day in Memoriam

Admirable and Gallant
In its history
All of our troops were valiant
Here and over seas
They made the sacrifice
To insure and secure
Our way of life and more
Through the decades
Throughout the centuries
Many spread over Arlington are laid
For all of us to see
As a reminder of what was done
And their price paid
For the freedom we have won

Now this tribute must endure the stain
Sullied by foot soldiers
Acting on trump's suggestions
Without a brain and without any questions
They marched One/Six/Twenty-One against
democracy
Breaching the Capitol Walls for all to see
Defiantly attempting to destroy an institution
That for good or for bad hadn't excluded them

Instead of asking those buried on the hill
If it might be better if they had just stood still
And asked about honor and the price they had paid
To build this democracy and the reasons it had stayed
And kept in reverence those who had gone to war
To preserve peace's principles which had simply gone ignored

gregoryedouglas
five/thirty/cleareyesight/plusone

My Favorite Things

Excerpts from Trump Tragedies

Handcuffs and shackles a bright orange suit
400 million owed, sexual offenses to boot
Firing your enemies and pardoning your friends
Tell me Donald when does this all end

We always thought that you'd skirt the law
But never on such a large scale as before
You'd open your mouth and everyone would run south
But now this time it's seriously in doubt

Covid Virus and Discrimination
Confederate Monuments aren't your admiration
Knee on Floyd's neck and his need to breathe
Your hesitance then silence were the signs to proceed

Everyone's good people in Charlottesville
Means white supremacists can live there until
Someone comes and puts down their foot
To establish these factions as real racist roots

Godfather, Czar, King or Monarch
Appears as the road you chose to embark
This is America the US of A, It's time to concede
So that you'll go away, and so will your greed

gregoryedouglas
eleven/nineteen/cleareyesight

I'm in a New York State of Mind...

(Premonition)

I guess if I were
The outer and inner complexion
Of Donald John Trump
I would have to Lie
I would have
All of my friends
To Lie
And my enemies as well
I'd hold more "Lie Rallies"
To convince my fan base
That my Lies held the truth
While identifying all truths
As the Lie WHAT??!
What Donald John has yet to realize
And refuses to dismiss is
That Lies accumulate Lies

With time Lies leave grimy
Soap scum and Bathtub rings
They are the embryos

That birth yellow filmy build-up
The jaundice that works into the fabric
Of inner and outer complexions
Time and aging lies have finality
And now coming into fruition
Aging and dementia
Have forfeited 45's assurances
That there will not be
Any loud clanging noises
Or conjoined metallic echoes
Reverberating up through the floors
And down that long narrow hallway
Each and every time his cell door closes...

gregoryedouglas
eleven/sixteen/cleareyesight

The Sunken Sonnet

Humpty Trumpty sat on the wall
Humpty Trumpty had a great fall
He was cracked from north to south
But no one could ever shut his mouth

He thought from his post that he was king
And from that wall could do anything
His only problem was Trumpty forgot that fall
And as cracked as he was he couldn't rule at all

With only his mouth being in the best of its
condition
He lied about the election to all who'd listen
Many believed him from near and far
And tried to re-raise their fallen star

But once Trumpty's shell was permanently broke
Everything else went up in smoke- And cannabis is
legal now!

gregorye.douglas
eleven/eighteen/cleareyesight/plusone

Historical Perspective

The Only Reason
History Might Say
That America
Was Blessed
With Donald Trump
Is To Insure
That Democracy
Will Never Ever Again
Be Stumped
Be Stunned And Stunted
Almost Into Extinction

gregorye.douglas
twelve/twenty-one/cleareyesight/plus one

The Waste Land

word hoarders

the inventors of verbosity

breed fictitious and caustic inaccuracies

that rage like a great desert storm

with her volume and acidic viability

solely entrusted to insure

that nothing but cactus

can grow...

gregorye.douglas
ten/nineteen/cleareyesight/plusone

White Out

still crippled
since setting foot upon this shore...

Mercy Dignity neither one
more humane if they used a gun
but bullets they will always save
no one kills a healthy slave
shackle him, muzzle him,
harness him too
train him to do what niggas do
head down and don't say a word
graveside tears are all they deserve

whatever "Lilly" told them he still doesn't know
each time seemed very different though
nebulous scenarios with different words
no actual accounting of what occurred
what was reported or distorted wasn't clear
but when a white girl cries out from fear
everybody is willing in fact to act "Still"
to the very same tears
that bludgeoned "Emmet Till"

gregorye.douglas
ten/nineteen/cleareyesight/plusone

Punished

Today,

The only reason why we

Have been allowed to live this long

Is in order that we may finally understand

Our sentence

We are here today

To witness the manifestations of

To feel the gravity of

And sense the actual burdens of

This unexonerated guilt...

gregorye.douglas
nine/twelve/cleareyesight

Day Watch

Life
is not short
it is long
and drawn out
exhausting and painful
awaiting applause for
the last breath's curtain call
to the drowning of the sun
and I have sat
and watched
for so long
cracked lips pressed
onto my windowpane
while thoughts
float down the river
in a rowboat
rudderless without oars
just counting the ripples
and waves
from dawn
to its dying into
the dead of night
I remove

the hearing aids
to shut out
the loud silences
of people
and places
that have
long since vacated

my porous recall
is not relief
it's just a flood
of forgetfulness
that drowns
my spirit
as I
sit here
swollen legs
cemented to
the floor
even weak and misting eyes
can see
that time and its
co-conspirator gravity
in their harvest
have stolen my strength

Life
is not short
it is long
and drawn out
exhausting and painful
as I strain
to find my feet
and with this
third leg in hand
hobble to the door
to greet you
with what is left
of the last
of the sunshine
in my smile

gregorye.douglas
eight/eight/cleareyesight/plusone

Reasons

(EWF)

The Reason Why I'm Writing Is
To Share With You This Gift Of Sight
That The Good Lord Has Given Me It Never Fails Even At Night
And With His Permission I'm In The Position To Share With You
What Is Seen And What Occurs Each Time You're In My View:

Oh, I've Seen Your Tilted Halo
And You've Walked With A Fractured Wing
Your Face Scrunches Up At Times
Because Shallow People Aren't Your Thing

You Thrive On Improvement
And With Scissors Paper And Glue
You Are Everyones "Mr. Fix It"
Making Everything You Touch Like New

Through Wars You Have Been
The Olive Branch And The Dove
Yet You Can't Accept
Are Blind And Don't Expect
What You Are And Do is Love

I'm Also Here To Inform You
God Will Adjust Your Halo
And Mend The Broken Wing
Because He Loves You So Very Much
And Angles Are Really His Thing

GOD BLESS

From A Room With A View

twelve/sixteen/cleareyesight/plus one

And The Band Played On

Mystic forces derailed the Hades Express
Where eventually I will rest
Though scarred and bloodied I should be
Buried in this history
Which viewed us as a people most proud
Never again would our heads be bowed
Jubilantly expounding upon "Black Power"
In confirmation of our finest hour

The fear and thrill of renaissance
Minus all; the ambiance
Music blaring and nostrils flaring
Dorms reeking of weed
Philosophizing about the struggle
And how we could succeed
Kent State's bullets in a hail
Students and demonstrators headed for jail

Attitude and aptitude kept the "pigs" in check
Fist raised as high as my Afro
Love beads about my neck
Clad in a dashiki and platforms
With others wanting to be
The Nigger – The Figure
The Mike Man – just like me
Power of the word
To be spoken
To be heard
To be jeered
To be hailed
For some to fight
For others to be jailed
Parents' pain – trailed their vacant looks
Drafted students don't need books

The reason for the riot

Some say yes, others deny it

Was in defiance

To proclaim

Our own self-reliance

I chose a conscientious war

Over the violent one

I chose the bloodless revolution

Over a country's mindless inclusion

I chose sanity

Over an insane number that could

Carry me to sea

And what in the hell were we fighting

And who was the enemy?

Martin, Jack, Malcolm and Bobby

Assassins camped out in the lobby

Leaders lost

Masses tossed

In an ocean of insanity

Questions on a nation's mind

Of them and thousands left behind

Many of which we could not find
Whose war had they died for?

And all the colors that went to fight
Returned to find injustice right
Where it had always been before
They went off to fight this war
Right at home and not next door

Many leaders sought political power
New factions formed by the hour
Many fizzled
Others lost force
I started riding that big white horse

Prestige's spotlight began to fade
As the mount increasingly weighed
Thundering through this blistered brain

The steed I felt I could restrain

Bucked me off again and again

This happened so repeatedly

I'd take my friends along to see

Many who'd ride along with me

From sugar to shit

From discrete to all over the streets

From an educated nigger

To how could you figure?

From smoking grass

To out on my ass

Drool dangling down my cheeks

Catatonic for several weeks

Crawling again then finding stride

Recuperating some pride inside

From a basement with crack

To struggling to get back

The concepts that were once me

The caring, the sharing and the dignity

Why me?

Why was I set free?

Others had fought this war

Some I had heard of

Many I had ignored

Some returned and others stayed

For some we dug an early grave

None would be honored at any parade

Why me?
Why was I set free?
My education didn't protect me
Did someone actually hear my plea
Or just select randomly?

From teacher to preacher
From sinner to winner

Me – the brother who had done it all
Me – the casualty who survived the fall
Me – the cosmic conduit
Surely they'd listen to avoid that pit
As I stood upon the stage
An ugly crowd became enraged
They didn't come to listen to me
They came to hear the beat you see...
And the band played on...

Denuding Redundancy

We are a generation of redundancies.
Like Trump, his followers are creatures of habit
who are destined to recreate their own demise. For there is no
place for progress when your backs and fronts are pinned up
against the Capitol Walls. This, from an attempt to oust
Democracy, in an all-out effort to raise the Devil's Demon,
Trump, as your banner; as your
second golden calf and as your cause...
But what of Christmas after New Year's Day?
Hasn't Santa gone away?
And are any of the girls or boys
afraid that Santa will take their toys???

Democracy be damned,
Trump plied them with the word elixirs causing
"his right" to rally and fight
while he hunkered down in his alley, out of sight until night,
being no bolder than the shrug of a shoulder
he said everything was all right.
Like the Charlottesville confrontation
he handed out commendations
that everyone was good, in broad daylight.

From the response from his throne,
they felt it good to go home;
after all they had done his bidding
But with their minds still up against that wall
The wall they cracked but didn't fall
Yes it was still there sitting
Where now was home without Democracy
And with just their leader trump to trust
In a moment's notice they all had to know
Their precious leader would always throw
All of them under the bus
Preserving himself as the upper crust
Of whom no one yet opposes
Yet certainly he's not Moses
Is this dessert again to be the desert for sure
Unless we decide against another encore
Of The Emperor Has on No Clothes

gregorye.douglas
one/five/cleareyesight/ plus two

Eventually

Time, Like God,

Becomes

The Judge...

AMEN

If I Should Die

Before I Wake

Finally

There Appears To Be

An Antidote

For The Kool-Aid...

Other Titles
By Gregory E. Douglas

COME MORNING

978-0-967312-37-8

Born of both fantasy and imagination I am sure that as you read there will be no need to look any further than yourselves for the facts and the truths. There is always a smidgeon of fact in fiction; there is always a smidgeon of truth in a lie and there is always the darkness before, come morning. 64 pages

51

978-0-9832608-6-8

The present-day prizes and products that dwell within a poet's mind. 68 pages

CIRCULAR BREATHING

978-1-941859-14-8

Circular Breathing is a technique used by musicians who play wind instruments. Some musicians can hold musical notes for periods of time that seem to last almost forever. At times when the notes appear to be exhausted, they lose their enchantment and become eerie.

Incorporated herein are some people whose personas would never permit them to be escorted through a life of futility while others, just as notable, have succumbed to the process. Life's best notes are appreciated when they give us time to evaluate the quality of their movement and then anticipate the change as it segues. Life, vibrant life, thrives on activity, growth and community while existence may be nothing less than Circular Breathing that eventually segues into an agonal rhythm. 54 pages

TRILOGY OF THE BOOGE MEN

978-1-941859-78-0

A clever story about the boogie men in our lives, real or imagined. Dr. Gregory Douglas, a master of poetry, has begun to experiment with longer works of prose, tied together by a powerful theme. We hope this book will be the first of many of his books in this genre. 54 pages

ON THE OTHER SIDE OF THIS REALITY

978-1-941859-81-0

2020 : Reflections from a Covid-19 Spring and a Policing Protest Summer. Insightful thoughts by Dr. Gregory Douglas, as he takes up the issue of Donald Trump's handling of the novel coronavirus (Covid-19) and public reaction to the police murder of George Floyd in Minneapolis. The poet is in rare form and at his passionate best in this provocative and sometimes stunning work! 64 pages

order at www.pegasusbooks.net

from bookstore and Internet Retailers

www.ingramcontent.com/pod-product-compliance
Lightning Source LLC
LaVergne TN
LVHW050943080826
845145LV00004B/1389